P9-DUE-220

When I'm kind to people, they feel happy. Then I feel happy, too!

My Behavior
I Am Kind

Liz Lennon

SEA-TO-SEA
Mankato Collingwood London

It feels good
to be kind.

I share my toys with my sister.

Why?

My sister
likes my toys.

When I
don't share,
she is sad.
Sharing is kind.

When my friend is unhappy, I ask her why.

I try to cheer her up.

Caring about friends is kind.

I say, "**Please**" when I ask for something.

What do I say when I get it?

I say,
"*Thank you*"
when I get it.

"*Please*"
and
"*Thank you*"
show
I am kind.

Sometimes
I make a
mistake.
I make
someone
unhappy.

What do I do?

I say,
"Sorry."

Sorry means
I feel sad
about what
I've done.

I'm not
just kind
to people.

Animals need
kindness, too.

I am always
gentle with
our dog.

She likes
to be tickled
on her tummy!

The best way to
be kind is to try
not to hurt any
person or
animal.

I don't like being hurt and neither do they.

About This Book

Kindness, like so many other positive character traits, is something that children have to be taught. The aim of this book is to give you the opportunity to share and discuss different aspects of behavior and how we can be kind. Looking at and talking about the pictures is a good starting point. Here are a few talking points and ideas:

How we can be kind The book covers different ways we can be kind: sharing, being concerned about friends, saying please and thank you, saying sorry when necessary, and being kind to animals. What other ways are there? For example, playing fair in games, not leaving others out, and not saying unkind things behind someone's back.

Examples of kindness When you read about someone being kind or watch a movie where people are being kind, comment on it. Similarly, if you experience someone being kind around you, point it out and discuss with the child how it made you (or them) feel.

How does kindness make you feel? Can the child think of times when they have been kind recently? How did it make them feel? What about when others are kind to us? Are there times when they haven't been kind? What did they do? How can we make it right when we haven't been kind? Encourage children to find solutions to disagreements that don't involve hurting someone else's feelings.

This edition first published in 2013 by
Sea-to-Sea Publications
Distributed by
Black Rabbit Books
P.O. Box 3263, Mankato,
Minnesota 56002

Copyright © Sea-to-Sea Publications 2013

Printed in the United States of America,
North Mankato, MN.

9 8 7 6 5 4 3 2

Published by arrangement with the
Watts Publishing Group Ltd, London.

Library of Congress Cataloging-in-Publication Data

Lennon, Liz.
  I am kind / written by Liz Lennon.
    p. cm. -- (Little stars : my behavior)
  Includes index.
  ISBN 978-1-59771-409-9 (alk. paper)
  1. Kindness--Juvenile literature. 2. Children--
Conduct of life--Juvenile literature. I. Title.
  BJ1533.K5L46 2013
  177'.7--dc23

2011052739

Series Editor: Sarah Peutrill
Art Director: Jonathan Hair
Series Designer: Paul Cherrill
Picture Researcher: Diana Morris
Consultants: Karina Philip and Deborah Cox

Picture credits:
Shutterstock: Joy Brown 1, 8, 9; Elena Elisseeva
19t; grublee front cover, 3; Eric Isselée 19b;
JacksColdSweat 11; Petr Jilek 20; Morgan Lane

Photography 22-23; Larisa Lofitskaya 13; naluwan
18; Ami Parikh 4, 6, 7; paulaphoto 15; pprt 10; Jane
September 2; Zurijeta 17.

Every attempt has been made to clear copyright.
Should there be any inadvertent omission please
apply to the publisher for rectification.

RD/6000006415/001
May 2012